Antonio VIVALDI

(1678 – 1741)

Concerto for Treble (Alto) Recorder, Strings
and Basso continuo, RV 108
A minor / la mineur / a-moll

Edited by
Manfredo Zimmermann

DOWANI International

Preface

This volume introduces you to Antonio Vivaldi's Concerto RV 108 in A minor for treble (alto) recorder, strings and basso continuo. The concerto has been edited and recorded by Manfredo Zimmermann, professor of recorder at the Wuppertal Musikhochschule and a specialist in early music. Though not as difficult technically as Vivaldi's concertos for sopranino recorder, it is delightful to play – Vivaldi at his best. The piano reduction has been specially prepared for our volume by the pianist and arranger Gero Stöver.

The CD opens with the concert version of each movement (recorder and orchestra). After tuning your instrument (Track 1), the musical work can begin. Your first practice session should be in the slow tempo. If your stereo system is equipped with a balance control, you can, by turning the control, smoothly blend either the recorder or the harpsichord accompaniment into the foreground. The recorder, however, will always remains audible – even if very quietly – as a guide. In the middle position, both instruments can be heard at the same volume. If you do not have a balance control, you can listen to the solo instrument on one loudspeaker and to the harpsichord on the other. Having mastered the piece at slow tempo, you can practice the first and third movements at medium tempo. We have omitted the medium tempo for the second movement, which is already relatively slow in the original. Now you can play the piece with orchestra accompaniment at the original tempo. At the medium and original tempos, the accompaniment can be heard on both channels (without recorder) in stereo quality. Each movement has been sensibly divided into subsections for practice purposes. You can select the subsection you want using the track numbers indicated in the solo part. Further explanations can be found at the end of this volume along with the names of the musicians involved in the recording. More detailed information can be found in the Internet at www.dowani.com. All of the versions were recorded live.

We wish you lots of fun playing from our *DOWANI 3 Tempi Play Along* editions and hope that your musicality and diligence will enable you to play the concert version as soon as possible. Our goal is to give you the essential conditions for effective practicing through motivation, enjoyment and fun.

Your DOWANI Team

Avant-propos

Cette édition vous présente le concerto pour flûte à bec alto, cordes et basse continue RV 108 en la mineur d'Antonio Vivaldi. Manfredo Zimmermann, professeur de flûte à bec au Conservatoire Supérieur de Wuppertal et spécialiste dans le domaine de la musique ancienne, a édité et enregistré ce concerto. Le niveau technique de cette œuvre est moins élevé que les concertos pour flûte à bec piccolo. Néanmoins, il est très plaisant à jouer – un vrai Vivaldi. La réduction pour piano a été réalisée par le pianiste et arrangeur Gero Stöver.

Le CD vous permettra d'entendre d'abord la version de concert de chaque mouvement (flûte à bec alto et orchestre). Après avoir accordé votre instrument (plage N° 1), vous pourrez commencer le travail musical. Le premier contact avec le morceau devrait se faire à un tempo lent. Si votre chaîne hi-fi dispose d'un réglage de balance, vous pouvez l'utiliser pour mettre au premier plan soit la flûte à bec, soit l'accompagnement au clavecin. La flûte à bec restera cependant toujours audible très doucement à l'arrière-plan. En équilibrant la balance, vous entendrez les deux instruments à volume égal. Si vous ne disposez pas de réglage de balance, vous entendrez l'instrument soliste sur un des haut-parleurs et le clavecin sur l'autre. Après avoir étudié le morceau à un tempo lent, vous pourrez ensuite travailler le 1er et le 3ème mouvement à un tempo modéré. Le 2ème mouvement n'est pas proposé dans un tempo modéré, car son tempo original est déjà relativement lent. Vous pourrez ensuite jouer directement le tempo original avec accompagnement de l'orchestre. Dans ces deux tempos vous entendrez l'accompagnement sur les deux canaux en stéréo (sans la partie de flûte à bec). Chaque mouvement a été divisé en sections judicieuses pour faciliter le travail. Vous pouvez sélectionner ces sections à l'aide des numéros de plages indiqués dans la partie du soliste. Pour obtenir plus d'informations et les noms des artistes qui ont participé aux enregistrements, veuillez consulter la dernière page de cette édition ou notre site Internet : www.dowani.com. Toutes les versions ont été enregistrées en direct.

Nous vous souhaitons beaucoup de plaisir à faire de la musique avec la collection *DOWANI 3 Tempi Play Along* et nous espérons que votre musicalité et votre application vous amèneront aussi rapidement que possible à la version de concert. Notre but est de vous offrir les bases nécessaires pour un travail efficace par la motivation et le plaisir.

Les Éditions DOWANI

Vorwort

Mit dieser Ausgabe präsentieren wir Ihnen das Konzert für Altblockflöte, Streicher und Basso continuo RV 108 in a-moll von Antonio Vivaldi. Manfredo Zimmermann, Professor für Blockflöte an der Musikhochschule Wuppertal und Spezialist für Alte Musik, hat das vorliegende Konzert herausgegeben und eingespielt. Dieses Konzert von Vivaldi ist technisch weniger anspruchsvoll als seine Konzerte für Piccoloflöte, aber trotzdem wunderbar zu musizieren – ein typischer Vivaldi. Der Pianist und Arrangeur Gero Stöver hat den Klavierauszug zu dieser Ausgabe erstellt.

Auf der CD können Sie zuerst die Konzertversion eines jeden Satzes anhören (Altblockflöte und Orchester). Nach dem Stimmen Ihres Instrumentes (Track 1) kann die musikalische Arbeit beginnen. Ihr erster Übe-Kontakt mit dem Stück sollte im langsamen Tempo stattfinden. Wenn Ihre Stereoanlage über einen Balance-Regler verfügt, können Sie durch Drehen des Reglers entweder die Blockflöte oder die Cembalobegleitung stufenlos in den Vordergrund blenden. Die Blockflöte bleibt jedoch immer – wenn auch sehr leise – hörbar. In der Mittelposition erklingen beide Instrumente gleich laut. Falls Sie keinen Balance-Regler haben, hören Sie das Soloinstrument auf dem einen Lautsprecher, das Cembalo auf dem anderen. Nachdem Sie das Stück im langsamen Tempo einstudiert haben, können Sie den ersten und dritten Satz auch im mittleren Tempo üben. Beim zweiten Satz haben wir auf das mittlere Tempo verzichtet, da er im Original schon relativ langsam ist. Anschließend können Sie sich im Originaltempo vom Orchester begleiten lassen. Die Begleitung erklingt im mittleren und originalen Tempo auf beiden Kanälen (ohne Blockflöte) in Stereo-Qualität. Jeder Satz wurde in sinnvolle Übe-Abschnitte unterteilt. Diese können Sie mit Hilfe der in der Solostimme angegebenen Track-Nummern auswählen. Weitere Erklärungen hierzu sowie die Namen der Künstler finden Sie auf der letzten Seite dieser Ausgabe; ausführlichere Informationen können Sie im Internet unter www.dowani.com nachlesen. Alle eingespielten Versionen wurden live aufgenommen.

Wir wünschen Ihnen viel Spaß beim Musizieren mit unseren *DOWANI 3 Tempi Play Along*-Ausgaben und hoffen, dass Ihre Musikalität und Ihr Fleiß Sie möglichst bald bis zur Konzertversion führen werden. Unser Ziel ist es, Ihnen durch Motivation, Freude und Spaß die notwendigen Voraussetzungen für effektives Üben zu schaffen.

Ihr DOWANI Team

Concerto

for Treble (Alto) Recorder, Strings and Basso continuo, RV 108
A minor / la mineur / a-moll

A. Vivaldi (1678 – 1741)
Piano Reduction: G. Stöver

DOW 2511

Recorder

Concerto

for Treble (Alto) Recorder, Strings and Basso continuo, RV 108
A minor / la mineur / a-moll

I ②

A. Vivaldi (1678 – 1741)

DOW 2511

2

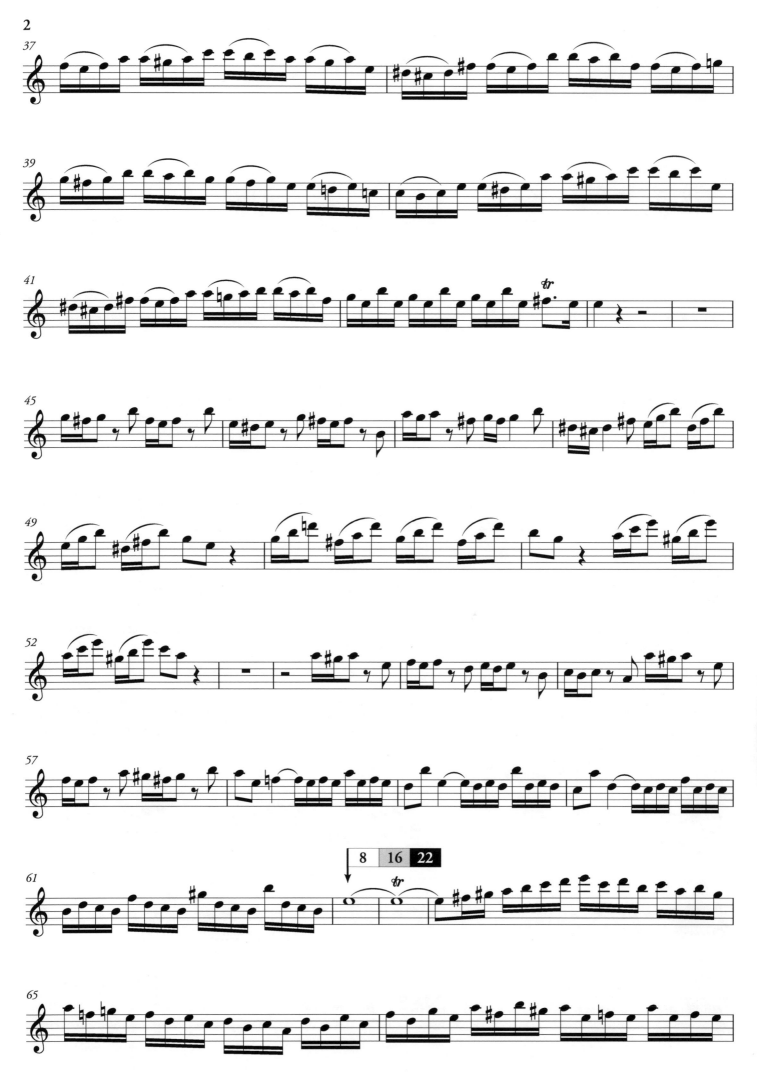

10

ENGLISH

DOWANI CD:
- Track No. 1
- Track numbers in circles
- Track numbers in squares

  | 1 | - tuning notes

  ● - concert version

  [□■■]

  - slow Play Along Tempo
  - intermediate Play Along Tempo
  - original Play Along Tempo

- Additional tracks for longer movements or pieces
- **Concert version:** recorder and orchestra
- **Slow tempo:** The recorder can be faded in or out by means of the balance control. Channel 1: recorder solo; channel 2: harpsichord accompaniment with recorder in the background; middle position: both channels at the same volume
- **Intermediate tempo:** harpsichord only
- **Original tempo:** orchestra only

FRANÇAIS

DOWANI CD :
- Plage N° 1
- N° de plage dans un cercle
- N° de plage dans un rectangle

  | 1 | - diapason

  ● - version de concert

  [□■■]

  - tempo lent play along
  - tempo moyen play along
  - tempo original play along

- Plages supplémentaires pour mouvements ou morceaux longs
- **Version de concert :** flûte à bec et orchestre
- **Tempo lent :** Vous pouvez choisir – en réglant la balance du lecteur CD – entre les versions avec ou sans flûte à bec. 1er canal : flûte à bec solo ; 2nd canal : accompagnement de clavecin avec flûte à bec en fond sonore ; au milieu : les deux canaux au même volume
- **Tempo moyen :** seulement l'accompagnement de clavecin
- **Tempo original :** seulement l'accompagnement de l'orchestre

DEUTSCH

DOWANI CD:
- Track Nr. 1
- Trackangabe im Kreis
- Trackangabe im Rechteck

  | 1 | - Stimmtöne

  ● - Konzertversion

  [□■■]

  - langsames Play Along Tempo
  - mittleres Play Along Tempo
  - originales Play Along Tempo

- Zusätzliche Tracks bei längeren Sätzen oder Stücken
- **Konzertversion:** Blockflöte und Orchester
- **Langsames Tempo:** Blockflöte kann mittels Balance-Regler ein- und ausgeblendet werden. 1. Kanal: Blockflöte solo; 2. Kanal: Cembalobegleitung mit Blockflöte im Hintergrund; Mitte: beide Kanäle in gleicher Lautstärke
- **Mittleres Tempo:** nur Cembalo
- **Originaltempo:** nur Orchester

DOWANI - 3 Tempi Play Along is published by:
DOWANI International
A division of De Haske (International) AG
Postfach 60, CH-6332 Hagendorn
Switzerland
Phone: +41-(0)41-785 82 50 / Fax: +41-(0)41-785 82 58
Email: info@dowani.com
www.dowani.com

Recording & Digital Mastering: Wachtmann Musikproduktion, Germany
Music Notation: Notensatz Thomas Metzinger, Germany
Design: Andreas Haselwanter, Austria

Concert Version
Manfredo Zimmermann, Treble (Alto) Recorder
Telemannisches Collegium Michaelstein

3 Tempi Accompaniment
Slow:
Mechthild Winter, Harpsichord

Intermediate:
Mechthild Winter, Harpsichord

Original:
Telemannisches Collegium Michaelstein